serenity

Dedicated to,
Yusra & Eiman

serenity

poems

F. S. YOUSAF

Andrews McMeel
PUBLISHING®

contents

I –*acceptance*

Many come and go, but you know all of me, and
your arms resemble a home for my soul.

All my life, I was searching for just this—acceptance and love.
Many times, I was given maps and hints of where to find it, and
only through hard work and determination would I come out
with being accepted. But I was exhausted after the fact—my knees
would refuse to stand straight; my eyes would not open with ease.

When I found the people who were right for me and did
not have to run in circles for their love and acceptance,
that is when I knew I was in good hands.

ONE GUARANTEE IN LIFE

The love you have given
trembles throughout my body—
forcing me to my knees
in a heartfelt contemplation.

For me,
the sun would not rise.
The nightly dew would go nowhere—
the plants would always weep.
And I would be alone
in a place I do not know.

You have given me reason,
a purpose.
That if all else fails,
I will always have you to cherish me.

A SMILE AS BRIGHT AS THE SUN

The thought of your smile—
the one that was personally sculpted for this earth.
One which turns the heads of flowers away from the sun
so they can get a peek.
It is a pot filled with holy water
to shower upon sown seeds,
and one which knows where to get me when I feel
as if
I do not know where to take my next steps.

ONLY US

Fall with me today
in waters so deep
that darkness steals the color off of us.
Let's become one, a blank slate.
No differences gripping us to what
we have always been
and that which made us.

We are whole together.
A masterpiece we both
choose to create and thus, become.

Fall with me again
as you lock into my fingers,
this time into luscious prairies.
For we know that there is no one
else in this world
but us.

DOSES OF MEANING

When I am with you,
things will feel easier.
I won't have to wait to see your face,
drive hours or catch flights
just to feel the peace you carry.

Bad days will still exist,
like rain on sunny days
or cold winds with the coming of spring.
But with those bad days comes an embrace,
your head fitting into my neck as if it
were sculpted just for you, and only you.

With that embrace comes meaning:
perhaps this world deserves me;
perhaps I am not as small as I thought.

SIMPLICITY

You have looked at me
when no one else had.
The sun tenderly taking hold of me
after a long absence
and when I am in dire need of its warmth.

In those moments, life does not seem as complex.
That everything under the deep blue sky
can fit in my palms.

GIVING TO EACH OTHER

You have seen me like no one else has,
and while that frightens me
enough to distance myself,
I know that your love for me
is as boundless as the skies—
as is mine for you.

EVAPORATION

A divide as big as oceans
can come between us,
so vast that the very thought of it
can seem overwhelming.

I know what lies in both of us—
in the passing time
we will work to make those oceans
into rivers, and then soon after, puddles.

The separation will only be worth a step,
close enough to where we can share an embrace.

WELLS OF PURITY

Days with you feel as if they are never-ending.
The sun stays out until the moment you turn your back to leave.
When we sit together, and you gently grab my hand,
slowly interlocking each and every finger as if both of us were
made of glass.
It is as if it is a droplet of Zamzam in a glass full of darkness—
putting ounces of purity to that which does not deserve it.

I don't tell you this often, but I should—
the love you have shown me makes me weep.
The younger selves who are trapped within me
have never felt that warm embrace.
They have only known what to be afraid of
and to love those who would hurt them.

And yes, while loving does bring pain,
I know that loving you
will be a certain step
to finally begin healing.

MEANING OF DESTINY

I do not fear death taking one of us,
for I am certain
that the goodbye will only be temporary.
It will be the same
as the way when we leave one another
and know
that we will eventually be reunited another day.

We will know for certain,
like the way the sky is always blue,
the sun always rising,
and the moon guiding lost souls in the darkness.

We know for certain
that no obstacle
can keep us apart for too long.

PRESENT-FORWARD

Between us, there are little moments of love.
A small hug shared
or the way you run your fingers through my thick hair.

The kind of moments that pull me to the present
and help experience the warmth of this world.

CLOSENESS

Your breath,
so light on my skin.
This calm everlasting—
at least until we say so.

GRATEFUL

It was marvelous
that I found my best friend
and soul mate
all in the same person.

BOND

We have a connection so pure
that love
has become an understatement.

CAPTURE

The first time we met
was as if the air stood still for brief moments.
Time was not moving forward—
life did not matter around us.
The only person who seemed to hold any weight for me
was you.

REMEMBRANCE

I am reminded by the love you carry
through your very thought of me.
The little moments when you make me feel a tad less alone
even though you are nowhere near me.

BRACE

You carried parts of me
that I had never discovered.
Almost every good aspect
which I possess today.

FAITH IN ONE ANOTHER

There have been moments of unclarity, uncertainty.
The way you feel when you're stuck at a crossroads,
not knowing which way is the right way,
not knowing what the way holds.

You cradle my ear
and whisper,

I will be here despite your failures,
just the way you will be here for me as well.

LET THE SUNLIGHT ENTER

Cherish the love that has held you down
through the storms of the night,
when even you felt like you would not make it through.
And when the sun shines valiantly,
you yourself know that

all is well
all is well
all is well

Cherish that love. Accept it as one you deserve.
Hold on to it, and never let that light dwindle.

FOR THE ONES WHO PICK US UP

For so long I have only let myself be burdened
with this weight on my chest and in my mind.
But lately, the heaviness that resides in me
feels lighter—

I find that it is always easier when
others help you carry the burdens
that live within us.

PARTNERSHIP

I want you
even in your sadness,
so you can heal
with me by your side.

BLOOMING

You gaze at me as if I am the best thing
to have happened to you.
Like my aura is life-altering,
and that your days would look
a bit dimmer without me.

No one has ever told me that before,
or made me feel as needed
besides you.

LETTING GO OF THE PAST

You have given me everything possible there is to give—
your body, emotions, mind, and more.
Yet I cannot seem to grasp it all.

I know this has more to do with me
and that I carry a deep unhappiness for myself.
One I must get over if I am able to fully appreciate your
beauty.

THAT WHICH I CRAVE

There is one thing I crave more than others.
The one that can brighten up my day and
make the world feel complete,
even if it is just for mere moments.
Lightning runs through me, and I feel alive,
so alive, more than I have ever been.

And that which I crave

is your smile.

DESERVING / UNDESERVING

I notice the way you look at me
and I cannot understand what you see.
I am all these terrible deeds wrapped in skin,
so difficult to love and someone who
does not deserve what you give.

But you do not see me
the way I see myself.

THE PAST IS THE BEST OF TEACHERS

People's words have strings attached to them,
and I've grown burnt out by
the many layers that lie beneath their intentions.

After peeling back those layers and learning
my lessons,
I've grown to know who truly loves me
and who desires to drain my will.

And I move forward with that knowledge.

THE GIFT

The laugh you've gifted me
has filled my body with solace.
Like when a lover hugs you,
their hands gently caressing the back
of your neck as if you're the only person
that's ever mattered in this world.

These days,
others have told me
that my laugh lights up rooms.

YOUR VOICE WILL HAVE A HOME

There are slight pauses in between
the words you speak.
The way wind howls during snowfall,
then nothingness until the next gust arrives.

Perhaps you were once told
that your voice does not matter—
you learned to strap a collar on it,
holding it back even when you did
not have to.

Having those unsaid words build a home in you
when you had no other room to spare.
But I am here now, I am here.
Your words will always have a place to go.
Your voice will always have a space to be heard.

WHEREVER THIS PATH MAY LEAD

I see you while the sun is rosy
and think of you
while the moon greets me
with a cool smile.
It's safe to say that I am growing
to love you more than ever before.
And I am not afraid to see where in the world
this love may take us.

FILLING THE VOID

My memories of you disappear
with the air that exits my lungs.
And I feel like a child
trying to imagine an event
that is yet to happen.

There is a lonely quality attached to this forgetfulness.
One which pushes me to see you more often
and to live full of life
in those very moments.

For when the memories depart,
I will know there are only
pleasant emotions behind
the vague memory of our day.

PRESENT LOVE

What I did not expect life to hand
me was a love worth cherishing
day in and day out.
Surely, I would be
long lost without it.

MESH

We have been knit,
you and I,
as if our colors
were meant to blend
to become a bigger picture.

LOVE THAT KEEPS ON GIVING

If you asked me to illustrate
an image of love,
I would not be able to.
The moments are too vast,

and only choosing one
would be an unjust action.

YOUR NAME MEANS EASE

I was once asked to breathe in peace,
to think of that which would
quell my heart
and create a sort of ease.
Of all that could have been thought,
you were the only ease that came to mind.

A LOVE SO WHOLE

I do feel incomplete,
but that is only with personal goals
and copious amounts of self-rejection.

Your love is not involved—
that aspect never lacks
at being fulfilled.

A BOND WITH LIGHT

We gather as the sun slowly disappears,
but I know the people I have surrounded myself with
will illuminate my surroundings.

WE SPEAK THE SAME

No matter the range that lay between
our (love) languages, I know, truthfully, our hearts
only call out for one another in the same dialect.

TRUST

Love is staying through the downfall,
the collapse, the absolute struggle—
believing the rise is on the way.

REFLECTIONS

You were more than just a person;
you became my mirror.
Correcting each other's ways every day
as we went along.
Neither of us was perfect,
but both of us were people
who would make one another
better in time.

WANTING NOTHING MORE

It was the happiness
in your eyes
that made me content,
a feeling I knew that nothing else could bring me.

A SOUND I RARELY HEAR

I struggle with accepting
the way you say my name.
So full of love—
a sound so foreign to my ears.

HOLD

You saw me broken, weak,
and in a place I had never been.
Yet, you stayed through it all.

RUSTLE

I am yours,

just as you have said the same about me.

This is an unnatural

yet elegant emotion which you have stirred within me.

SEPTEMBER 22, 2016

I came early in the morning, earlier than I needed to,
just to spend some time with you.
You were in the city for class, anyways.
So why not make a date out of it.

We navigated around the subways,
you teaching me the ropes as we went along.
I had barely any experience in the city,
and you basically called it home.

We walked across Washington Square Park
and sat on a bench right across from a playground.
The fall breeze was slight,
and there was no need for layering.

You held my hand as I held yours.
We drank coffee and took pictures.
Some of the sights, but mostly of each other.
I could not let this day go;
I did not know when I would see you again.

We traveled and walked
all the way to Central Park
and sat under a tree
after I was swindled by a panhandler.
I am not proud to admit that I was naive,
but doing so helps me for future encounters.

We talked a bit more
and held tighter than before.
We knew our day together was ending
and that we would not see each other
for quite some time.

The breeze was simple,
and the day cool.
If only you knew how much I think of it,
you would call me a fool.

II – *hope*

Look forward to tomorrow, for it will undoubtedly
be more meaningful than today.

Hope is an ever-changing word. It constantly fleets but knows where its home is and eventually returns. I've dealt with the fluctuation behind it, myself. There are some days in life when it feels like the sun will never come out again, and other days when there is nothing but love and light in the air. Despite it all, we are here, and we deserve to be here. Regardless of the negative way we feel at times.

ONE WITH THE MOON

I imagine our souls
meeting under a tree
in the midst of fall
so the moon can have a front-row seat to see our performance.

We dance to offbeat tunes
till our legs drop from beneath us.
Sweating, breathing so heavily
that the grassy fields sway
with each exhale.

And your head pressed against my chest,
a slight movement when my heart thumps.

When the light reaches over our eyes,
you fleet with the night.
And I solemnly walk across the prairie
wondering when I may see you again.

NATURE'S CALLING

It is the light from your eyes
that wakes me as if it is a fiery sunrise.
Canaries and bluebirds sing throughout the skies,
the calm and tranquility of dawn holds no lies.

Speak to me, tell me how morning dew rests on your skin.
How trees weep whenever they hear your voice,
flowers dance with the wind when you come across them.

Tell me how nature planted itself in you.
Sow seeds into me
so I may learn to grow as well.

STRIVE

I cannot show you how
the future will unfold,
but I can promise you
that all we go through
will be worth it.

SERENDIPITY

How much of a coincidence
could it be
that when I yearned for the best to happen,
you appeared right in front of me?

SURMOUNT

How remarkable is it
that beautiful, vibrant days
always follow gloomy ones.
We are constantly reminded
that the good parts in life
will always outshine the bad.

AMBITION

What's the reason you keep on living?

Because there may be happiness
written for me tomorrow,
and if not tomorrow,
then perhaps the day after.

EYE-CATCHING

You have seen all which
frightens you, yet you still stand.
Making sure the world sees you.

THE GOOD WILL PREVAIL

There was a reason for everything—
it was to bring you back home.
To show you that the good still remains,
towering over the bad.

Always.

THE THOUGHT OF YOU

I don't know why
I kept on going
when the world gave up on me,
but the thought of you
made me feel at peace.

BELONG

I am destined to be here,
to belong to the ground
that is beneath my feet.
And to be with those
who cherish me.

WHAT WE CALL HOME

I always recall the days we spend
in each other's worlds.
It is an entirely different view for me,
and one which I know can
help me learn so much
about what we choose
to call home.

YOUR JOURNEY IS NO ONE ELSE'S

There is so much that passes by me
that I feel as if I am missing out.
Life moves so quickly, and it doesn't intend to slow down.

I have learned
that despite how fast others are going,
the only pace that matters is yours.

No one else has lived or will live
the life you carry.

LET YOUR SOUL SPEAK

There are moments where I am stopped—
I forget the right way to go
and even contemplate retracing my steps.
To go back to where I used to be
in order to figure out
where exactly I desire to go.

I like to tell myself that regression is normal.
A delicate part of life.
A cloth with two sides:
one which can be used as a stepping-stone
for improvement,
or one where you can easily become
trapped in the past.

I take the steps back
in order to move forward.
We must learn how to love ourselves generously,
for only then
may we learn more about our souls
and where we truly desire to go.

ENDURANCE

Despite how much you have been hurt
and have lost,
know that the sunrise looks different every day—
that all the difficulties will fade away

in time. All good in this world takes time.

MINDFULNESS

In the periods where life
does not go in my favor,
I remind myself that though
this is a place I do not want to be,

I will not jail myself
with the hopes
that this spell ends soon.

Push yourself to make the most
of what has been placed on your path.
Know how fruitful life can be
after this time.

YOU WILL FIND YOURSELF

There have been many moments
where I believed my life would stop moving.

To be stuck in place,
in purgatory between what I do not know
and what I have always lived through.

And I am afraid of this in-between.
To not rise or fall—
forward or back.
My foot stuck in wet cement beside
ongoing traffic,
all moving along while I do not.

Rivers flow,
clouds graze.
Despite how slow they go,
they all move to where they need to be.

Perhaps I will as well.

GLORY OF SPARE MOMENTS

There have been many moments where I struggle to look up. Where I can't see the end to all the tests being thrown my way. I am hollowed out by screams and shouts of "keep on going" and "the struggle will end."

I question if it will. Truly, I do. So much of my young life I have felt like it wouldn't. Days and weeks would pass, and absolutely nothing would feel different. I would be on a roller coaster, loop after loop. My mind tired, my body numb. The mental exercises to make sure I was going to make it through each and every day were tiresome and excruciating.

I have collapsed many times. I can't even count on my fingers and toes on how many it has been anymore. And I know it's so hard to get back up. I've been on that very same ground you may find yourself time after time.

I know that while it may seem difficult, that things may not entirely get better with a snap of a finger or a season's end—with patience, the tangles will unwind. I will find how to feel whole for spare moments in time.

CREATE

How beautiful it is
that though you may not wholly know
the purpose of your life,
you have so much time
to construct one for yourself.

MENTALITY

All my life, I never carried much importance for myself.
A bystander—one who would pedestal everyone's happiness
so far above their own
that worth becomes others' currency.
Expendable, and temporarily dependable.

It has taken years to unravel this gift—
the deserving to be loved and cared about without worry.
To be with those who can call you their sanctuary

and you, them.

DEAR: ME

There are wounds that lie deep,
a seabed / caverns and craters where others
do not attempt to go into, for they may become lost
like the various fond memories you once carried.

It may be time to begin healing, no?
Why live in pain when there are remedies to help
with the tragedies
where you may have been too young to know how they would
affect you lifetimes later.

What's the worst that could come out of closing
that which still causes you to tear—
to question your very own life?

No soul deserves to live with those brittle aches,
so, ask yourself,

why should yours?

A FIRE FROM OTHERS

I will give you love
even on days I do not feel it for myself.

I know that though
it is nonexistent in my being,
others will warm me up
until I know I matter as well.

PILLARS

I always struggled with finding
those who would hold me up
when all was falling.

My support beams
and those who would make sure
I was not collapsing in on myself
as they laughed and cried away.

And while I do not have that right now,
I know I will find
those who are made for me
when the time is right.

EMBODYING ART

There are days I do not feel as if I am living;
instead, an existent being walking the various streets of life—
not noticing all which surrounds them.

And as much as I believe
that this leads me to be broken,
I have to realize that this life is long,
and to feel so many different emotions
on a daily basis is normal.

It helps remind us that we are human,
beings who are not perfect
but doing the most to be the best for this world

and for ourselves.

IN TOW

You will be yourself again one day,
but it takes time to pick up all the pieces.
I'll be by your side through it all.

REFUGE

Even though you are far gone,
I still carry an ache—
the itch to feel your warmth.
To know how sanctuary in oneself may feel again.

And I acknowledge that
I will slowly make my way
back to you.

PERSIST

There may be days
filled with plenty of rain
and ominous clouds.
No matter how long they last,
parts of me know that they are temporary.

Life goes on, and I will go on as well.

REASONS

Live,
so you can tell
your story of survival
to those who need it most.

TENACITY

You have felt what it is like
to be at the bottom.
How cold it feels, and how alone you might be.
How the world constantly moves forward despite
you not being able to,
how the skies still shine blue,
but you not being able to take in its beauty
each and every day.

You have felt what it's like to be at the bottom—
know all the good you feel now
is because of your perseverance.

FEARS THAT LINGER

My greatest fear is not losing you—
our names are etched in stone
that cannot be altered.

My greatest fear is becoming
the person that has shown me all
the ways to not treat someone.
One that has hurt me,
has made me carry a burden
so heavy that my bones groan
with each step I take.

My greatest fear is losing who I am—
the person you have loved.
And in turn, becoming a stranger to you and myself.

LEARNING MOMENTS

We are filled to the brim with shortcomings.
We make mistakes, we do not understand
one another at times,
and there are plenty of moments
when we are not graceful.

And though we may grow to despise ourselves
for all that we've done in the past,
the faults we create become our greatest teachers.

We learn to become better
for one another as the days pass.

INTRUSIVE THOUGHTS

Layer after layer I peel,
searching for an emotion that I know
I should be feeling instead of this—

The desperation to run
to a place where not a soul knows me.
To scratch my skin until it breaks
or my nails fall off, whichever happens first.
To shut down. Crack. Break under the overwhelming
weight of life and the transition to adulthood.

Darling,
under all these levels, these layers,
I am unequivocally excited for the future.
But my mind wanders to all the bad that may occur.
And the stress of these thoughts, the guilt of them,
at times is too much to handle on my own.

I've overheard that these what-ifs only plague us
so we can effectively combat these situations
if they do happen.

WITH FIRE COMES REBIRTH

There were a handful of moments
where I believed I felt
flowers rising in me.
A forest being nurtured in between
the spaces of my ribs.
But before they could mature,
a match paired with a gust of wind would be forced
into my ever-growing nature,
causing wildfires even I could not contain.

With the pyre came a void which refused to grow.
That's what I presumed my worth to be
in the hands of one who did not deserve me.

Until one stepped onto that barren land
and planted their own bushel.
Which sprouted life across the plain.
A forest which ran wild to grow
into all it ever needed to be.

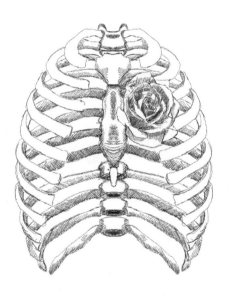

FULL OF LIFE

I will choose my own road,
one which does not carry your remnants.
One where your ashes have not touched.
This is my own journey,
my story,
and I intend to make it memorable.

TAWAKKUL

While I carry many moments of doubts,
I also have plenty of hope
that I will one day understand your existence,
and I will know mine as well.

SUFFICIENT

My body is slowly becoming
what it used to be—
rebuilding bones precisely,
with fragments of past trauma
and a hopeful future.

A holy vessel,
one I must take care of now more than ever.

When your unsolicited words strike my skin,
they become dust.
The kind you see in air in between the rays
of sunshine that disappear as your day goes on.
Almost an afterthought.

Your words do not affect me,
nor will they.
For I have already filled my body with enough air
that I don't find myself gasping
for a sliver of yours.

FLUX

The lonely nights become overshadowed
by the noises a sunrise brings with it.
The birds congregating,
car engines blazing,
and a bright light—
a sign of a new day
and a clean slate.

AVAIL

All this life I have lived,
despite the various downfalls,
has been forever worth it.

RECOGNIZE

I am not ungrateful
for all the opportunities
that you have given me,
but I am not grateful
for all you have put me through.

A ROCK AGAINST WAVES

For the majority of my life,
I wandered aimlessly—
filled with voided feelings.
Very rarely do I burst with emotion,
but when I do,
I notice that my heart softens.

TURBULENCE

Do not classify yourself
as a failure
when your future is delayed
by circumstances that are not
in your hands.

YOUR OWN PATH

I will not live
according to others' dreams
and aspirations.
Their life is their own—
subtle dust compared
to what mine will be.

STEADY

The next step is uncertain,
as I am free-falling into
a path different than my original.
I can only hope
to land on my feet
and be ready to move forward.

PEACE FINDS A WAY

There was a point
when I did not value my life.
And I attempted to find
any means to escape.
But there is a point where things began to get better,
and so, I waited.

PUSH FORWARD

Self-doubt is a fool
attempting to hold you back
from your true potential.

TAKE A CHANCE

I tell myself endlessly
that I am not capable,
but these are lies I fall into
because I am afraid
that there is a chance at failing.

REMIT

While there is still sadness in me,
there are also glimpses of happiness and light.
Moments I wish
and know
can return indefinitely.

III – *tranquility*

The destination is to find peace, but the journey
will show how much we will cherish it.

I ask myself a lot what tranquility truly is. Is it the way you feel when you're with the person who carries your heart? Or the way you feel when you're sitting on the beach, feet stuck deeply in the sand, and your mind is only filled with the breeze, the earth, and how peaceful life can truly be? It can be both of these things or neither of them.

I have learned that tranquility can be whatever you desire it to be.

MY SANCTUARY

The sun prancing through the window,
the fan grazing our bodies on low—
the slight tone of birds traveling home fills the air
and my nose pressed against your jaw.

I feel as if my heart is wrapped, cushioned so nothing
can get to it.
I may feel tranquil at the moment;
it has been a long day since I felt that.

EVERY FIBER AND OUNCE

Whenever my eyes land upon you,
it is as if all else fades away.
I see a warm light peeking over the horizon—
welcoming at the very sight, that I drag my body toward it.
Surely, one that makes me feel so gentle
should be given all of me.

SIMPLE MORNINGS

Years have stacked on each other.
This calm feeling has never lasted this long.
I am afraid it will be stolen at any moment.

The sun peers through the blinds,
a thin ray racing over your hands
as they rest on my chest.

Believing in this will make me turn my back
on what I have always known.

Perhaps it is time to do so.

A LOVE WHICH SOWS

Your fingers trace
the roots of my hair
as you tell me that lately
you have been seeing
flowers blooming through the pores
of my body.

I know
they would not have grown
without the very love you give.

SCATTER / SENSIBLE

There are some days
when I do not feel love.
As if it were stolen from my grasp,
and despite all my effort to find what was once mine,
I come up empty-handed.

The past is constantly standing behind me,
misplacing feelings and thoughts.

I have lived this hectic life for so long,
and it will take time for me
to become adjusted
to the peace you bring me now.

ALLY

You took my fears
as if they were your own.
My hand in your palms
as we walked across uncertainty.

HALLOW

Be patient
and learn the ways of your body.
Your soul is a guest
that calls your sacred vessel home.

INSIGHT

Being strong
is when you can cause harm
or hurt another,
but choose not to.

GLOOM

You have been there
when no one else was.
Reminding me that the sun will
always brighten my day.
Even when I feel clouds
hovering over me.

RENAISSANCE

There was once a week that felt like no other—
the sun and moon had been smiling at me,
blanketing me in a motherly embrace.

I felt life as if I were a child again,
looking out the car window on long road trips
and taking in all the nature around me.
Imagining racing against imaginary friends
as our car hopped from one goal to another.

There was not a worry in my mind, not a single stressor,
not even a thought.
I just knew, acknowledged, that I was fine.
Like the puzzle was whole,
all the pieces sitting flatly on the surface.

I hold that week close—
now I know what it truly means to be at peace.
Like the earth after rain,
a nation after its civil war.

OUT OF THE STORM

Life has its ups, downs, and its share of shaky moments,
as if it hits patches of strong wind—
in those moments I wonder if this is the end.

Or if it is just the beginning
of learning how to cherish
how to truly fly.
And acknowledging the ways of
our own freedom.

CLASP

Your laugh, cries, smile, and all
the moments we've spent together
are still on the surface of my mind.
I think about you even though you
are no longer nearby.

To be truthful,
the lasting thought of you
gets me through all the difficulties.

AUTONOMY

I feel terribly incomplete without you,
but know if I am to truly grow
that I must feel complete
without you.

HOMECOMING

I can wander
far from my origins,
far enough that one may
even lose sight of me.

But I know, despite how far I go,
I will be welcomed home
with open arms.

THE CALM NEVER WORE OFF

A peaceful silence—
horses grazing the land
and sheep running around.
There are no sounds of cars on the road,
only the wind rustling the trees and
the subtle chirp of birds.

Honey drips into the teacup,
the laughs of those who fill my mind
with nostalgic memories echo through my body.

All that has happened to me before seems meaningless.
For once, I know I am moving on
from living in the past.

GRAIL

There is only one tree I dream of—
whose branches spread so far and wide
that one can see it hundreds of miles away.
The tree that provides shade on harsh summer days,
and one that gives shelter when the weather worsens.

The tree that reminds me that I am home
when my eyes reach its core.
One which reminds me that I am living
and have made it to where I'd like to be.

CULTIVATING IN US ALL

The silence evaporates
like the blankets of snow at our feet.
With that cycle comes more life.
Whether that be nature, glorious in all its colors,
or the sound of footsteps on the street below.

A new beginning,
a kind where seeds are not only sown
in the dirt below,
but in us as well.
To grow with all
that will begin to grow around us.

BETWEEN YOU AND ME

There is a slight breeze where the ocean rests.
A sun slowly being covered
by blankets of waves.
The sky is ethereal,
a bucket of pink paint seemingly
falling from the heavens above.

And I,
standing in awe.
Toes buried in dust and history.
Feeling that all will be fine.
Wishing you could gaze
at this wonder by my side.

Another moment we can share between us
would be lovely, wouldn't it?

FIGHT FOR YOURSELF

It is a pleasant day for a rebirth,
wouldn't you say?

Come, take my hand.
The sun is not as harsh today,
and the night is not as dark.
Let us finally fight for who we aspire to be,
after all these years
of letting the hurt tell us who we are.

After all,
I have heard that you should fight for
those your heart belongs to—
and today is a pleasant day for that change.

EACH JOURNEY LOOKS DIFFERENT

This is the journey that was created for me.
For my eyes only—
for the world to run past me in its own way
which many may not understand.
For each sunrise and sunset
which others may not find view-worthy,
for the moments and memories which carve themselves
in my mind, and for the emotions
that only I get to feel,
and no one else.

THE BEST IS YET TO COME

Despite your touch being entirely absent from my skin,
I still feel hurt over leaving you looking through the window.
For we all must tear off our shackles of familiarity—
I do wish we could have
unlocked one another together.

FOR LIFE

The best of days / in your arms / your hands pressed against my back /
your eyes closed, taking in the warmth /
the sun peering through the clouds,
wondering where we have gone to / its eyes aching to see us /
to greet us / to celebrate us /
a letter resting at our feet / whispering into my ear that life would
not be as sweet if this bond did not exist.

THROUGH THE DARK

Lengthy night drives
to escape ourselves
just for an hour or two.
Filled with soothing tunes
and light conversations—
I wonder what they mean to you.

PEACE EXISTS IN YOU

When sadness strikes,
I look back and reminisce
over all the little things
that ignited some happiness in me.

And it comforts me to know
how much I can truly help myself.

THE PAST HOLDS NOTHING NOW

I always contemplate
all that could have been—
a new sun has risen
and my world is being held
by your smile.
A reminder
that I am only defined by the now.

ENTITLE

You deserve to reminisce about the past,
enjoy the present,
and be excited about the future.

ON TO BETTER THINGS

I used to obsess over
what you had done, and all the pain
that was committed against me.

After all this time,
you have become a rare thought,
one that barely gets the time of day.

AWARENESS

I always despised the notion
of letting go.
I let it simmer, enough to boil
me to a stand, but not enough to overflow.

Until one day I realized that I had lost control.
What I did not let go
spilled all over me—
enough for others to see
the wear and tear I had put myself through.

Enough for me to realize
that holding anger would not hurt another soul
but my own.

HEAD ABOVE WATER

I am constantly defeated by my own thoughts,
but I always tell myself that I am winning
for I am still here, thriving.

OBSTACLES

There is a pain in me,
but I do not allow that pain
to be a defining factor
of my being.

Just a minor part of me;
that which I must hurdle over.

PERFECTION IN A PERSON

Your embrace is filled with peace,
and I ask myself how this could
possibly get better,
and I know that it cannot.

This tranquility and solitude
is undoubtedly perfect.

TRAIN

We are meant to change.
This life is not made to be lived uninterrupted.
The challenge is accepting
that we cannot control
but learning how to tame the unknown.

CHANGE IS NEEDED

Salvaging love is a choice,
and it may not be as simple
as it seems.

Grow independently, figure yourself out—
examine every crack and layer beneath,
confront every shadow you hold, ask yourself
why it calls you home.

Do not go back the same person
you once were.

INDEX

Andrews McMeel Publishing
a division of Andrews McMeel Universal
1130 Walnut Street, Kansas City, Missouri 64106

www.andrewsmcmeel.com

23 24 25 26 27 VEP 10 9 8 7 6 5 4 3 2

ISBN: 978-1-5248-7103-1

Library of Congress Control Number: 2021945029

Editor: Patty Rice
Art Director/Designer: Diane Marsh
Production Editor: Thea Voutiritsas
Production Manager: Carol Coe

Cover illustration by Justin Estcourt
Interior illustrations by Syed Ali Saud

ATTENTION: SCHOOLS AND BUSINESSES
Andrews McMeel books are available at quantity discounts
with bulk purchase for educational, business, or sales
promotional use. For information, please e-mail the Andrews
McMeel Publishing Special Sales Department:
sales@amuniversal.com.